Guess What!

Activity Book 1

with Online Resources

British English

Susan Rivers

Series Editor: Lesley Koustaff

CAMBRIDGE
UNIVERSITY PRESS

Shaftesbury Road, Cambridge CB2 8EA, United Kingdom

One Liberty Plaza, 20th Floor, New York, NY 10006, USA

477 Williamstown Road, Port Melbourne, VIC 3207, Australia

314–321, 3rd Floor, Plot 3, Splendor Forum, Jasola District Centre, New Delhi – 110025, India

103 Penang Road, #05-06/07, Visioncrest Commercial, Singapore 238467

Cambridge University Press & Assessment is a department of the University of Cambridge.

We share the University's mission to contribute to society through the pursuit of education, learning and research at the highest international levels of excellence.

www.cambridge.org
Information on this title: www.cambridge.org/9781107526952

© Cambridge University Press & Assessment 2016

First published 2016

40 39 38 37 36 35 34 33 32

Printed in Malaysia by Vivar Printing

A catalogue record for this publication is available from the British Library

ISBN 978-1-107-52695-2 Activity Book with Online Resources Level 1
ISBN 978-1-107-52691-4 Pupil's Book Level 1
ISBN 978-1-107-52827-7 Teacher's Book with DVD Level 1
ISBN 978-1-107-52696-9 Class Audio CDs Level 1
ISBN 978-1-107-52697-6 Flashcards Level 1
ISBN 978-1-107-52698-3 Presentation Plus DVD-ROM Level 1
ISBN 978-1-107-52799-7 Teacher's Resource and Tests CD-ROM Levels 1–2

Additional resources for this publication at www.cambridge.org/guesswhat

Contents

Hello!

1 Look and match.

1

a

b

2

c

3

d

4

2 Ask and answer with a friend.

1 Hello, I'm Mandy. What's your name?

2 Hello, I'm Jack.

3 This is Penny.

4 Hello Penny.

3 **Listen and stick.**

4 **Listen and number.**

a

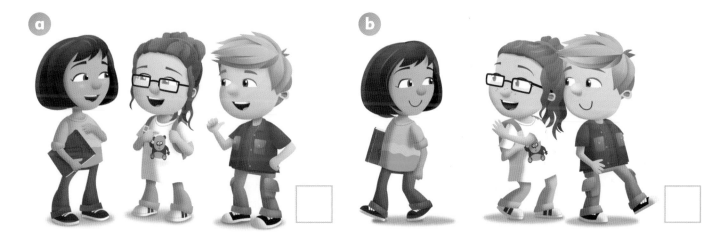

b

c

1

5 (Think) **What's next? Draw a line.**

1 | 2 | 4 | 6 | 2 | 4 | 6 | 2 | 4 | ←

10

2 | 8 | 9 | 10 | 8 | 9 | 10 | 8 | 9 | → 6

3 | 3 | 5 | 7 | 3 | 5 | 7 | 3 | 5 |

4

4 | 6 | 5 | 4 | 6 | 5 | 4 | 6 | 5 |

3

5 | 1 | 8 | 3 | 1 | 8 | 3 | 1 | 8 |

7

6 (CD1 11) **Listen and write the numbers in the pictures.**

1

2

3

4

7 **Listen and colour.**

1

2

3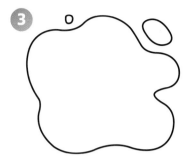

4

5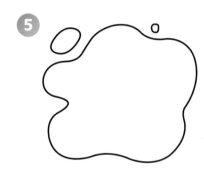

6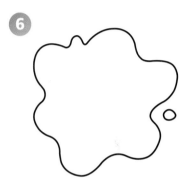

8 (About Me) **Look. Then draw and say.**

1

2

How old are you?

What's your favourite colour?

I'm ...

My favourite colour's ...

My picture dictionary Go to page 84: Tick the words you know and trace.

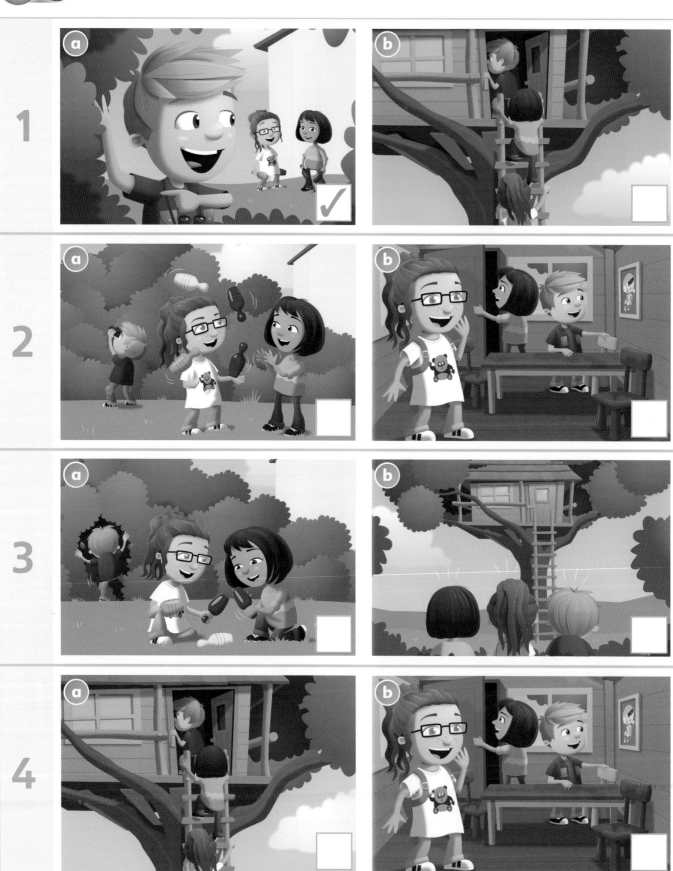

10 What's missing? Look and draw. Then stick.

a

b

c

I'm curious.

11 Trace the letters.

A pink and
purple panda.

12 Listen and circle the *p* words.

1  2  3  4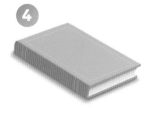

What colour is it?

1 CD1 21 **Listen and colour.**

2 **Look and colour.**

  **+**  **=**

 **+** **=**

 **+**  **=**

Evaluation

1 Follow the lines. Then trace and say.

a David

b Olivia

c Leo

d Tina

2 What's your favourite part? Use your stickers.

story   song   video

3 Puzzle Trace the colour.

pink

Then go to page 93 and colour the Hello! unit pieces.

1 **CD1 25** Listen and tick ✓.

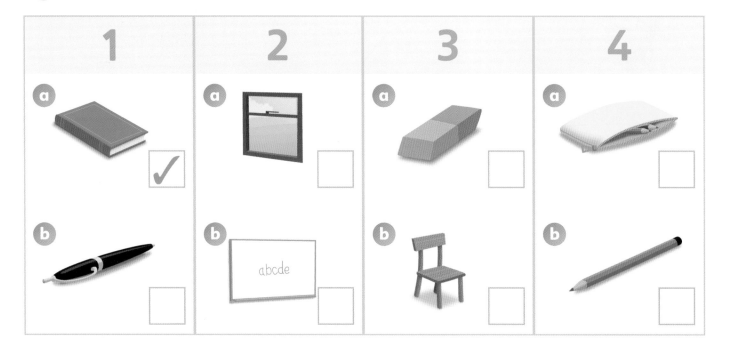

2 Look and match.

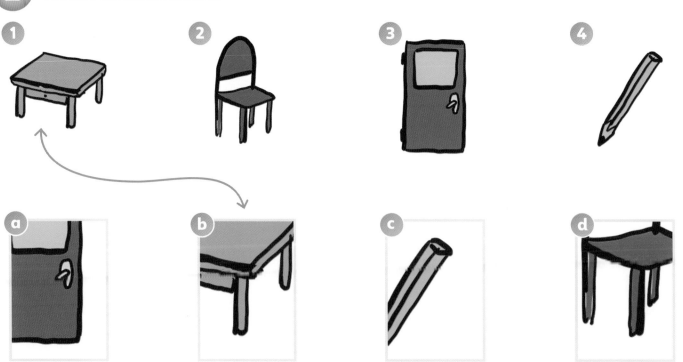

3 (CD1 27) **Listen and stick.**

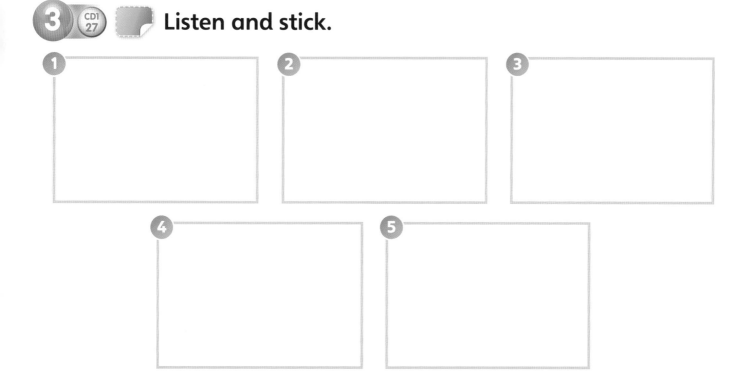

1
2
3
4
5

4 (Think) **What's next? Draw a line.**

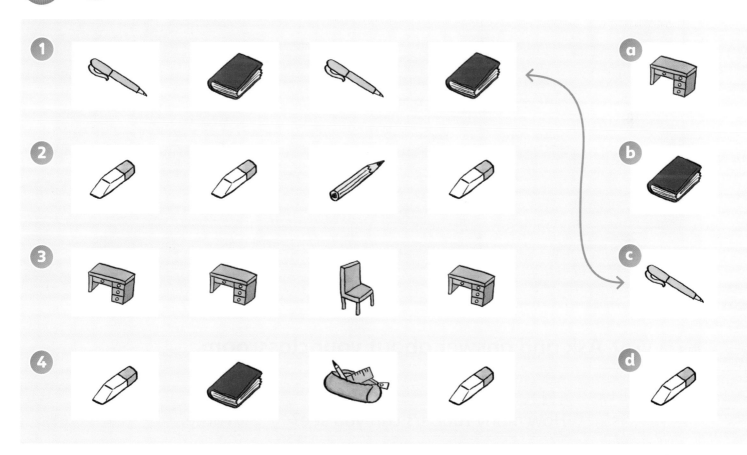

My picture dictionary → Go to page 85: Tick the words you know and trace.

Vocabulary **13**

5 Look and count. Write the number.

2

---

6 Ask and answer about your classroom.

How many rubbers can you see?   Three.

7 CD1 32 **Listen and tick ✓ or cross ✗.**

1

✗

2

3

4

8 Think **Circle the different one.**

1 **a**  **b**  **c**  **d**

2 **a** **b**  **c** **d**

10 **What's missing? Look and draw. Then stick.**

I'm friendly.

11 **Trace the letters.**

A bear with
a blue book.

12 CD1 37 **Listen and circle the *b* words.**

1

2 abcde

3

4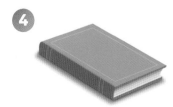

Value   Pronunciation: *b*   **17**

What **material** is it?

1 Look and match.

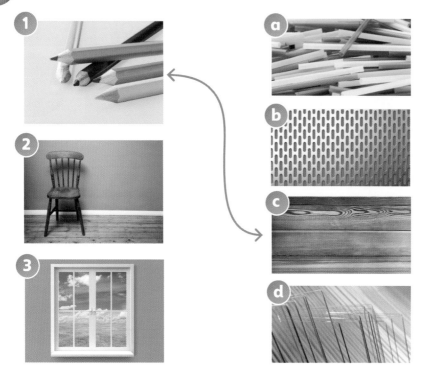

2 (CD1 39) Listen and tick ✓.

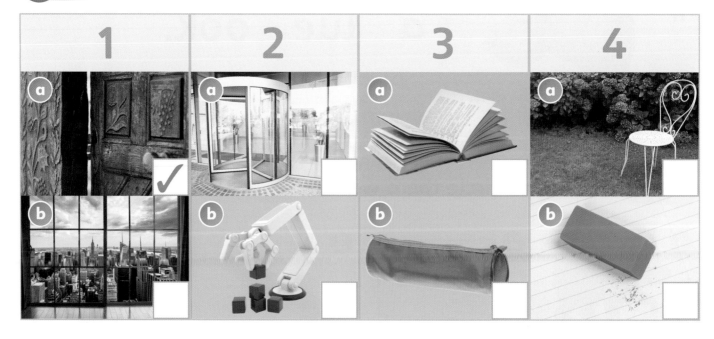

Evaluation

1 Look and trace. Then say.

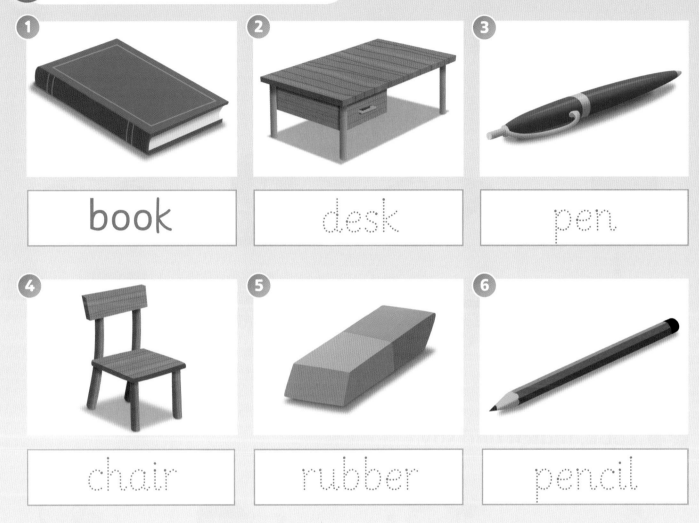

1 book

2 desk

3 pen

4 chair

5 rubber

6 pencil

2 What's your favourite part? Use your stickers.

story   song   video

3 Puzzle Trace the colour.

red

Then go to page 93 and colour the Unit 1 pieces.

2 Toys

1 **CD1 43** Listen and tick ✓.

1	2	3	4
a ✓	**a**	**a**	**a**
b	**b**	**b**	**b**

2 Look, match and say.   1 kite

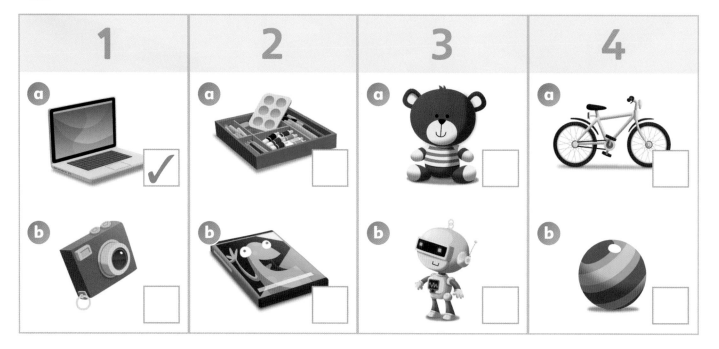

3 **Listen and stick.**

1

2

3

4

5

4 (Think) **Look and circle the toys.**

My picture dictionary → Go to page 86: Tick the words you know and trace.

Vocabulary **21**

5 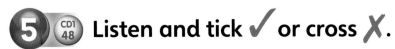 **Listen and tick ✓ or cross ✗.**

1 ✓

2 ☐

3 ☐

4 ☐

6 (About Me) **Draw your favourite toy and say.**

What's this?

It's a …

7 **Listen and number the pictures.**

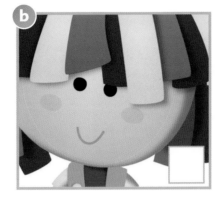

1

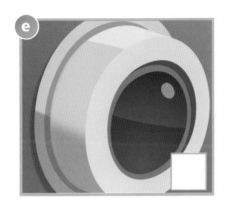

8 **Listen and draw the pictures.**

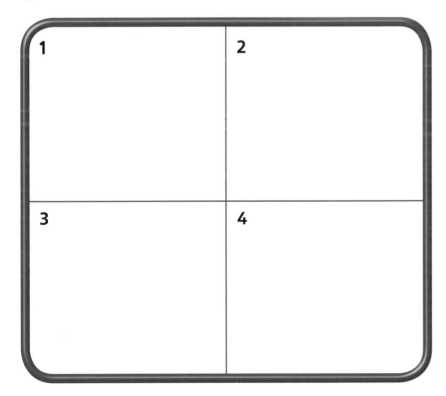

1

2

3

4

1

a ✓

b

2

a

b

3

a

b

4

a

b

10 **What's missing? Look and draw. Then stick.**

I'm polite.

11 **Trace the letters.**

A turtle with two teddy bears.

12 CD1 56 **Listen and circle the *t* words.**

1

2

3

4

Is it electric?

1 CD1 58 **Listen and tick ✓ (electric) or cross ✗ (not electric).**

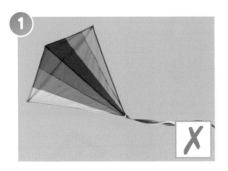
✗

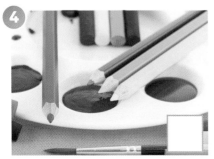

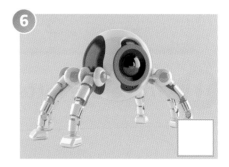

2 **Look at Activity 1 and draw.**

Electric	Not electric
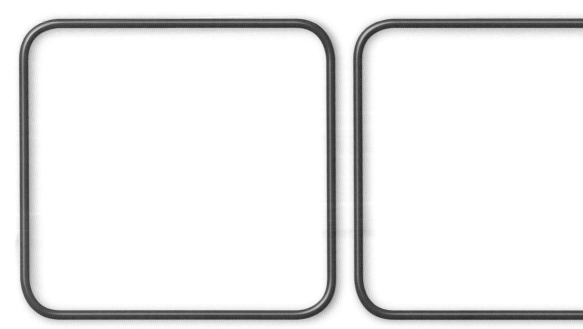

Evaluation

1 **Look and trace. Then say.**

1

kite

2

robot

3

ball

4

bike

5

doll

6

camera

2  **What's your favourite part? Use your stickers.**

story   song   video

3 **Puzzle** **Trace the colour.**

green

Then go to page 93 and colour the Unit 2 pieces.

Review Units 1 and 2

1 Look and say. Find and circle.

2 CD1 60 Listen and number the pictures.

a)

b)

c)

d)

1

e)

f)

7

3 Family

1 Trace the words and match.

1. **mum**
2. **dad**
3. **sister**
4. **brother**
5. **grandma**

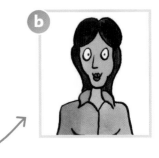

2 Look and write the number.

1 cousin   2 uncle   3 grandpa   4 aunt

3  **Listen and stick.**

| 1 | 2 | 3 | 4 | 5 |

4 Think **Read, look and tick ✓.**

1. dad ☐ ☐ ✓

2. aunt ☐ ☐ ☐

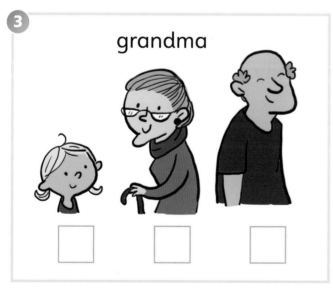

3. grandma ☐ ☐ ☐

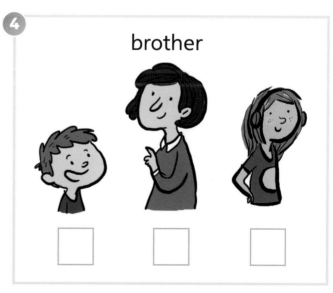

4. brother ☐ ☐ ☐

My picture dictionary → **Go to page 87: Tick the words you know and trace.**

5 Look, read and match.

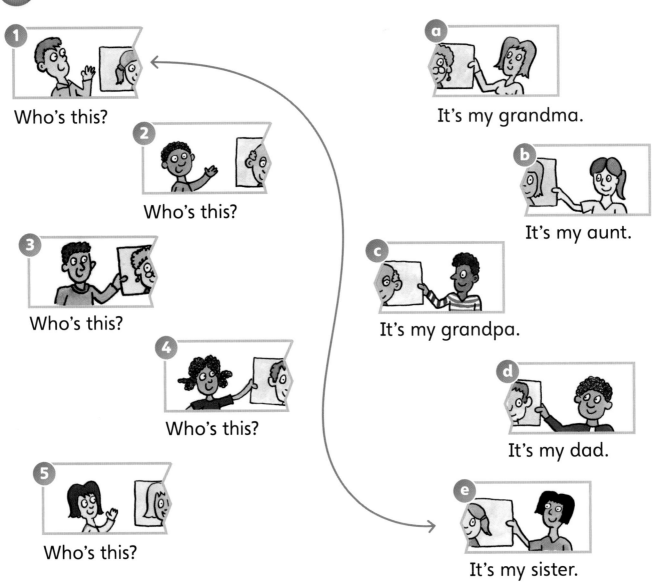

1. Who's this?
2. Who's this?
3. Who's this?
4. Who's this?
5. Who's this?

a. It's my grandma.
b. It's my aunt.
c. It's my grandpa.
d. It's my dad.
e. It's my sister.

6 (About Me) Draw a member of your family. Then ask and answer with a friend.

Who's this?

It's my ... .

Listen, read and tick ✓.

1

my brother ☐

my cousin ✓

2

my mum ☐

my aunt ☐

3

my mum ☐

my grandma ☐

4

my sister ☐

my cousin ☐

5

my cousin ☐

my aunt ☐

6

my dad ☐

my uncle ☐

8 **Look, read and circle the correct word.**

1 Who's **this** / (**that**)?
It's my uncle.

2 Who's **this** / **that**?
It's my cousin.

3 Who's **this** / **that**?
It's my grandpa.

4 Who's **this** / **that**?
It's my sister.

10 **What's missing? Look and draw. Then stick.**

I love my family.

11 **Trace the letters.**

A dolphin in a red desk.

12 **Listen and circle the *d* words.**

1

2

3

4

What continent is it?

1 **Listen and write the number.**

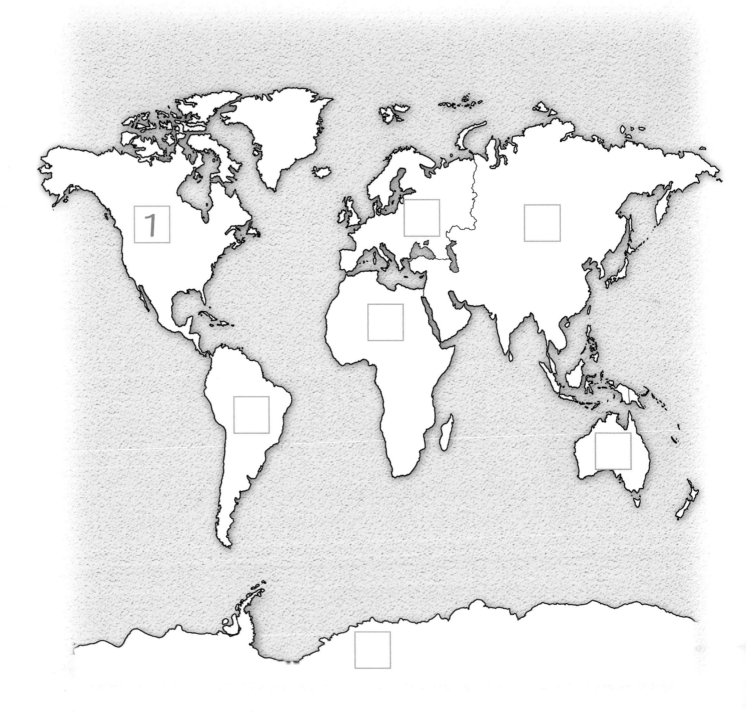

2 **Look at the map again. Listen and colour.**

Evaluation

1 Read and trace. Then circle and say.

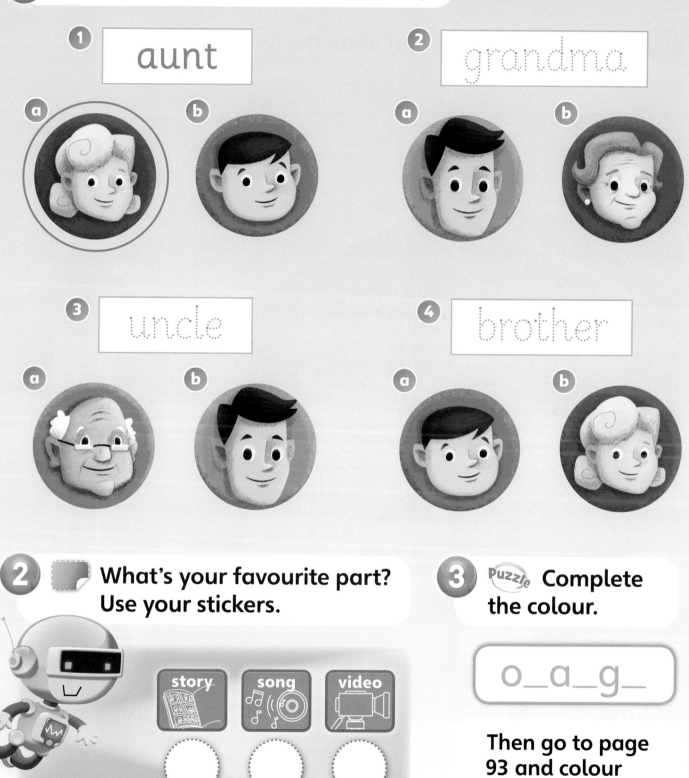

① aunt

② grandma

③ uncle

④ brother

2 What's your favourite part? Use your stickers.

story song video

3 Puzzle Complete the colour.

o_a_g_

Then go to page 93 and colour the Unit 3 pieces.

At home

1 Look at the picture and write the letter.

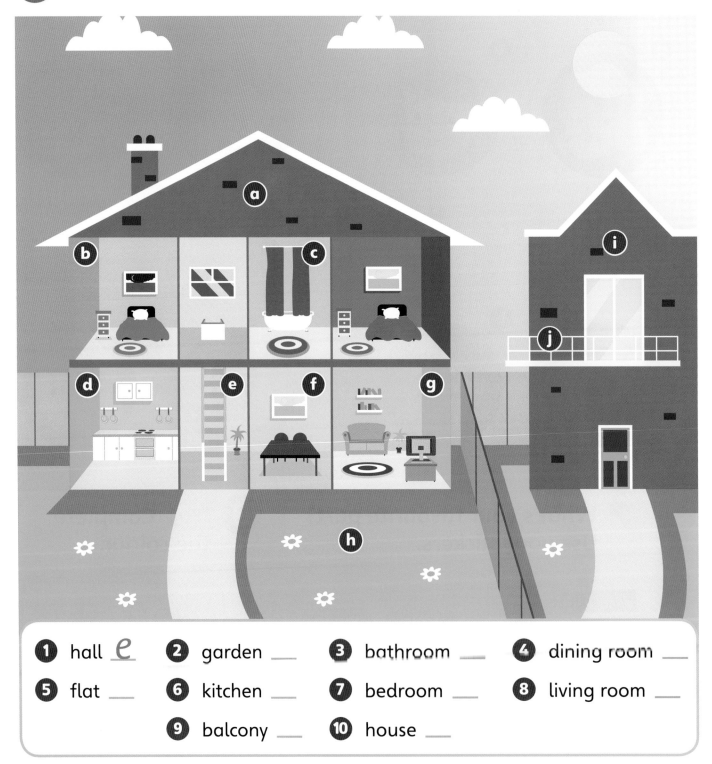

1 hall *e* **2** garden ___ **3** bathroom ___ **4** dining room ___

5 flat ___ **6** kitchen ___ **7** bedroom ___ **8** living room ___

9 balcony ___ **10** house ___

2 Listen and stick.

1	**2**	**3**
4	**5**	**6**

3 Look, read and circle the correct word.

1 (kitchen) / dining room

2 hall / living room

3 bedroom / balcony

4 kitchen / bathroom

5 hall / garden

6 balcony / dining room

My picture dictionary Go to page 88: Tick the words you know and trace.

4 (Think) **Look, read and match.**

1
Where's your aunt?

a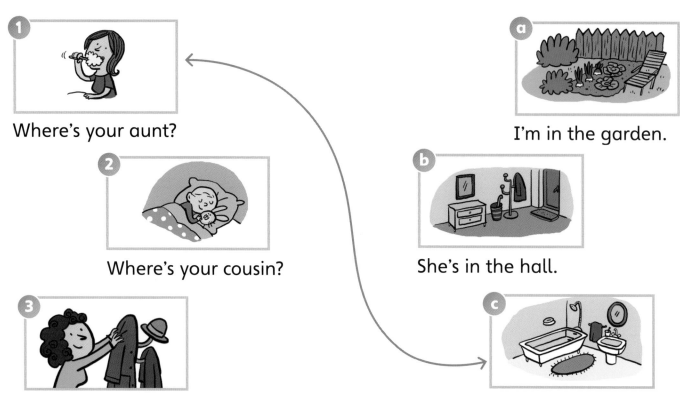
I'm in the garden.

2
Where's your cousin?

b
She's in the hall.

3
Where's your mum?

c
She's in the bathroom.

4
Where are you?

d
He's in the bedroom.

5 (About Me) **Draw yourself. Ask and answer with a friend.**

Where are you?

I'm in ...

6 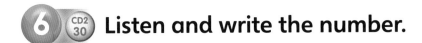 Listen and write the number.

①
②
③
④
⑤

7 Draw the objects in the picture. Ask and answer.

Where's the _____ ?   It's _____ ?

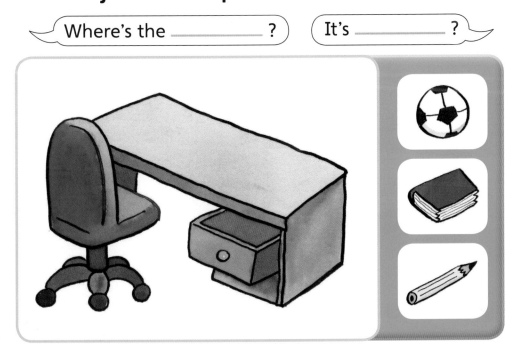

8 CD2 32 Listen and number.

a

b

c **1**

d

e

f

9 **What's missing? Look and draw. Then stick.**

I look after things.

10 **Trace the letters.**

An ant with an apple.

11 CD2 35 **Listen and circle the *a* words.**

1   **2**   **3**   **4**

What shape is it?

1 **Look and colour the shapes.**

2 **What's next? Match, then draw and colour the shapes.**

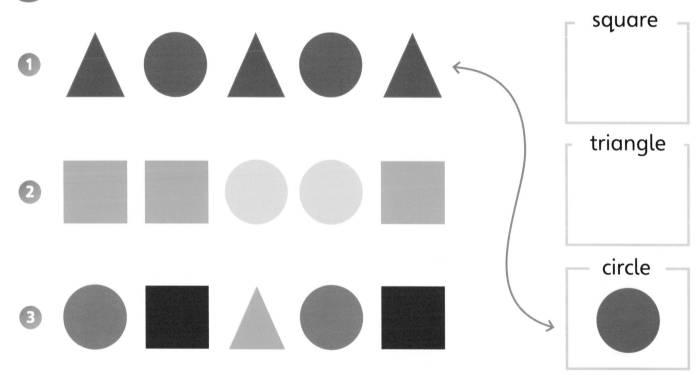

square

triangle

circle

Evaluation

1 Read and trace. Then circle and say.

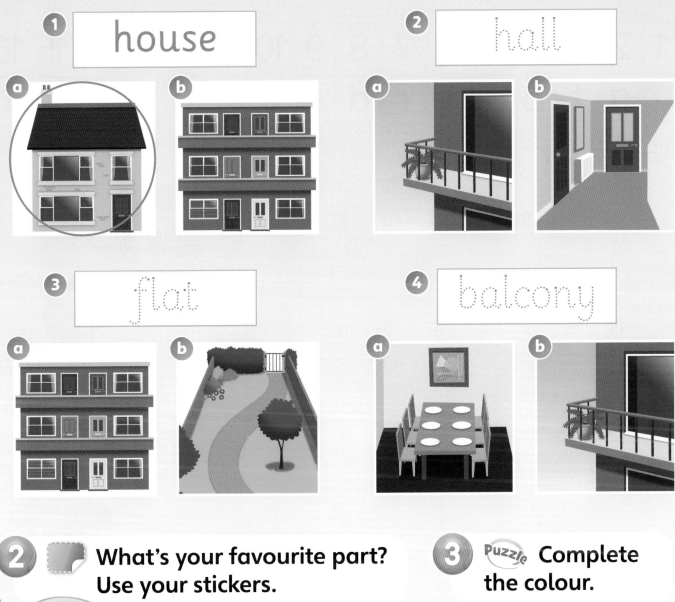

① house
② hall
③ flat
④ balcony

2 What's your favourite part? Use your stickers.

story   song   video

3 Puzzle Complete the colour.

y_l_o_

Then go to page 93 and colour the Unit 4 pieces.

Review Units 3 and 4

1 Write the words and match.

1	2	3	4	5	6	7	8	9	10	11	12	13	14	15	16
u	a	t	b	s	c	r	d	o	e	n	g	m	h	k	i

1
b r o t h e r

4 7 9 3 14 10 7

2
_ _ _ _ _ _ _

15 16 3 6 14 10 11

3
_ _ _ _ _ _ _

12 7 2 11 8 13 2

4
_ _ _ _ _ _

12 2 7 8 10 11

5
_ _ _

8 2 8

6
_ _ _ _ _

14 9 1 5 10

a
b
c
d
e
f

2 **Read and match the questions with the answers.**

1 Where's the computer? _c_   **a** She's in the living room.
2 Is that your cousin? ___   **b** No, it isn't. It's my sister.
3 Who's that? ___   **c** It's on the desk.
4 Where's your mum? ___   **d** It's my sister.

3 **Circle the correct words and write.**

mum   bedroom   grandma   ~~under~~

1

What's / Where's the doll?
It's _under_ the bed.

2

Who's / Where's this?
It's my _____ .

3

Who / Where are you?
I'm in my _____ .

4

Is that / Who's your aunt?
No, it isn't. It's my
_____ .

1 **Read and circle the correct word.**

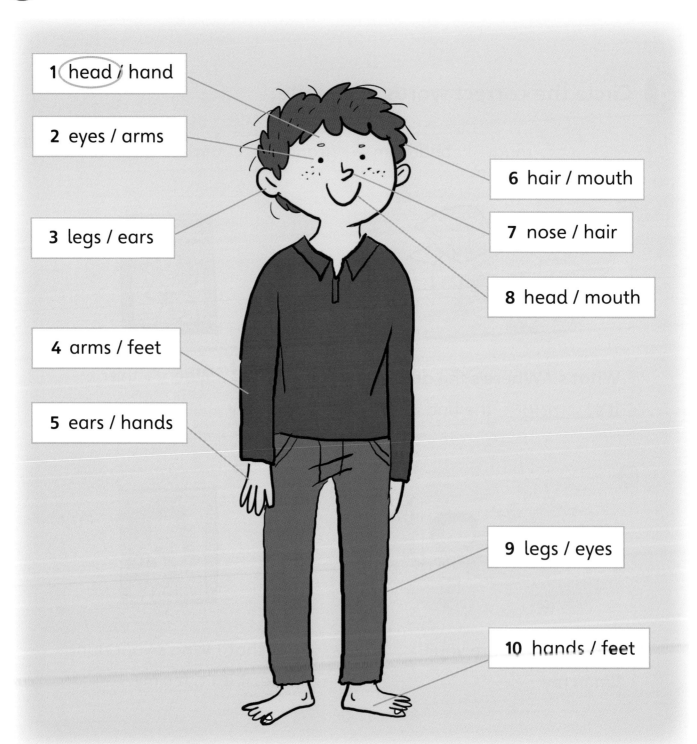

1 (head) / hand

2 eyes / arms

3 legs / ears

4 arms / feet

5 ears / hands

6 hair / mouth

7 nose / hair

8 head / mouth

9 legs / eyes

10 hands / feet

2   **Listen and stick.**

1	2	3

4	5	6

3 **Look at the picture. Find and circle the words.**

h	e	a	d	e	p	n
l	e	g	l	a	l	o
h	h	k	o	r	j	s
a	a	e	r	t	y	e
i	r	w	h	a	n	d
r	m	o	u	t	h	n
q	n	v	f	e	e	t

My picture dictionary → Go to page 89: Tick the words you know and trace.

4 (CD2 45) **Listen and tick ✓.**

5 (Think) **What's different? Circle the word.**

(eyes) / ears

feet / hands

legs / arms

mouth / nose

6 Look, read and tick ✓.

Have you got hair?

| | Yes, I have. | ✓ | No, I haven't. |

Have you got two arms?

| | Yes, I have. | | No, I haven't. |

Have you got four legs?

| | Yes, I have. | | No, I haven't. |

Have you got one nose?

| | Yes, I have. | | No, I haven't. |

7 (About Me) **Draw a robot. Then complete the sentences.**

I've got _____

_____ .

I haven't got _____

_____ .

8 CD2 48 **Listen and tick ✓.**

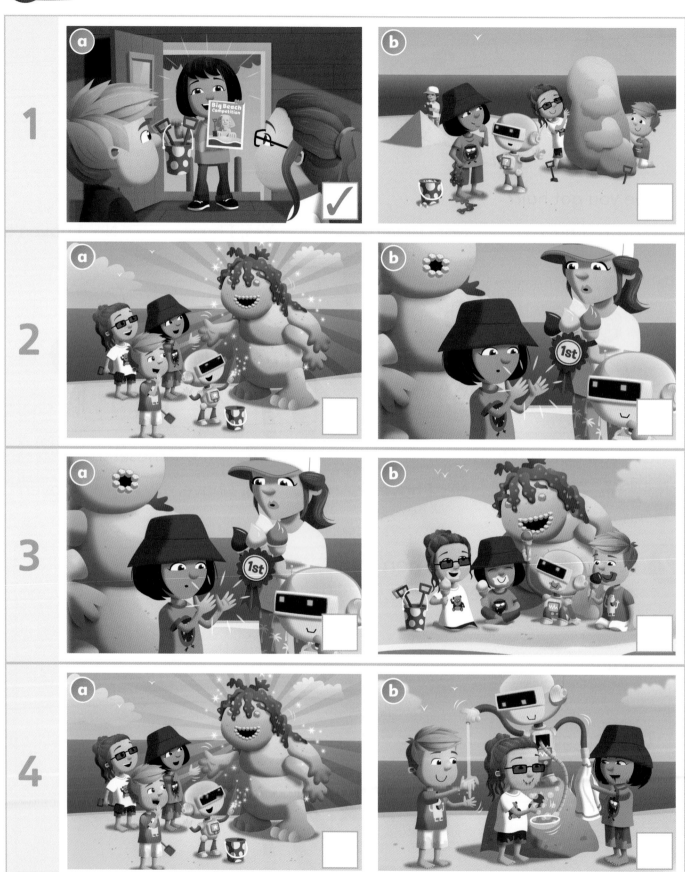

9 **What's missing? Look and draw. Then stick.**

I'm clean.

10 **Trace the letters.**

An iguana
with pink ink.

11 CD2 51 **Listen and circle the *i* words.**

1  **2**   **3**   **4**

What sense is it?

1 **Look, read and match.**

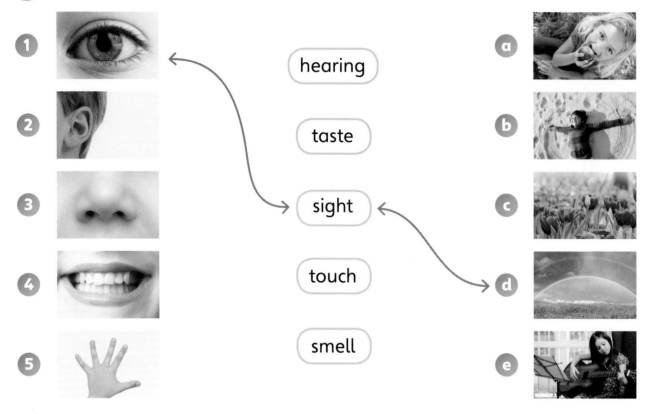

1

2

3

4

5

hearing

taste

sight

touch

smell

a

b

c

d

e

2 **Look and tick ✓.**

	👁	👂	👃	😁	✋
	✓				

Evaluation

1 **Look, match and trace. Then read and say.**

head

feet

ears

nose

2 What's your favourite part? Use your stickers.

story   song   video

3 Puzzle Complete the colour.

b_u_

Then go to page 93 and colour the Unit 5 pieces.

6 Food

1 Look and write the word.

1
k m l i
milk

2
p e a l p
_____

3
g e g
_____

4
c e h s e e
_____

5
a e w r t
_____

6
a a a n n b
_____

2 Complete the words and match.

1 jui_c_e   **2** o _ a n g e   **3** b _ e a d   **4** c _ i c k _ n

a    **b**    **c**    **d**

3   **Listen and stick.**

1

2

3

4

4 Think **Look and write the words.**

~~cheese~~   an apple   juice   bread   water
a banana   an egg   an orange   chicken   milk

We eat ...

1 *cheese*

2 _____

3 _____

4 _____

5 _____

6 _____

7 _____

We drink ...

1 _____

2 _____

3 _____

My picture dictionary → Go to page 90: Tick the words you know and trace.

5 **CD3 09** **Listen and tick ✓ or cross ✗.**

1			✓	✗
2				
3				
4				

6 **Look, read and circle.**

1  I like / (don't like) juice.

2  I like / **don't like** oranges.

3  I like / **don't like** bread.

4  I like / **don't like** water.

5  I like / **don't like** apples.

6  I like / **don't like** eggs.

7 Look, read and tick ✓.

1

Do you like bread?

[✓] Yes, I do. [ ] No, I don't.

2

Do you like eggs?

[ ] Yes, I do. [ ] No, I don't.

3

Do you like bananas?

[ ] Yes, I do. [ ] No, I don't.

4

Do you like juice?

[ ] Yes, I do. [ ] No, I don't.

8 (About Me) Look and answer the questions with *Yes, I do* or *No, I don't*.

1 Do you like chicken?

_____ .

2 Do you like milk?

_____ .

3 Do you like cheese?

_____ .

4 Do you like bananas?

_____ .

9 CD3 12 **Listen, look and match.**

10 **What's missing? Look and draw. Then stick.**

I'm patient.

11 **Trace the letters.**

An elephant with ten eggs.

12 CD3 15 **Listen and circle the e words.**

1

2

3

4

Where is **food** from?

 Look and tick ✓ or cross ✗.

Plants

Animals

② **Look, read and circle.**

1

(plant) / animal

2

plant / animal

3

plant / animal

4

plant / animal

5

plant / animal

6

plant / animal

Evaluation

1 **Look, match and write. Then read and say.**

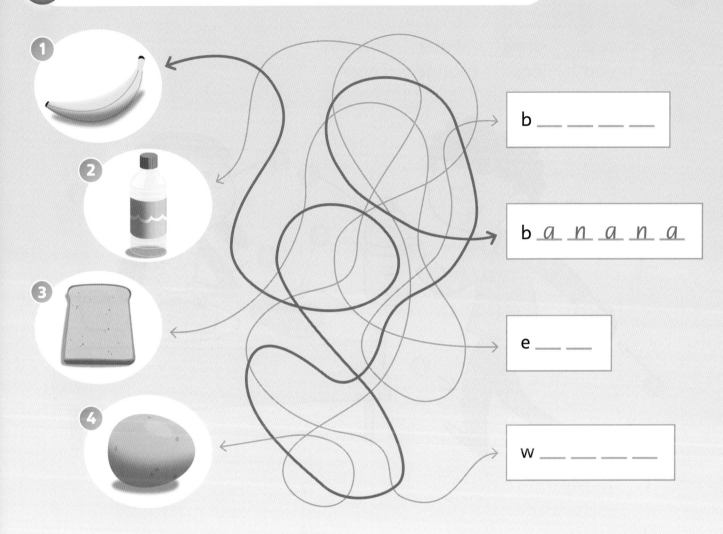

b _ _ _ _ _

b *a n a n a*

e _ _ _

w _ _ _ _ _

2 **What's your favourite part?
Use your stickers.**

story   song   video

3 **Puzzle** **Write the
colour.**

p e u l r p _ _ _ _ _

**Then go to page
93 and colour
the Unit 6 pieces.**

Review Units 5 and 6

1 Look and write.

cheese   ~~arms~~   water   mouth
bread   legs   orange   nose

1   _arms_

2 _____

3 _____

4 _____

5 _____

6 _____

7 _____

8 _____

2 Read and match.

1 I like   a   like juice.

2 I've got   b   two ears.

3 I don't   c   chicken.

4 I haven't   d   got two heads.

3 Write the question. Then tick ✓.

1

you / three / Have / got / hands?

<u>*Have you got three hands*</u>?

☐ Yes, I have.   ✓ No, I haven't.

2

like / eggs / you / Do?

_____

☐ Yes, I do.   ☐ No, I don't.

3

got / two / you / Have / ears?

_____

☐ Yes, I have.   ☐ No, I haven't.

4

you / Do / milk / like?

_____

☐ Yes, I do.   ☐ No, I don't.

1 **Look, read and circle the word.**

1

swim / (sing)

2

climb / paint

3

dance / draw

4

ride a bike / play football

2 **Look at the pictures. Find and circle the words.**

1

2

3

4

5

6

runswimjumppaintclimb(dance)

3 CD3 22 **Listen and stick.**

1

2

3

4

5

6

4 Think **Read and circle the object.**

1 dance

2 draw

3 sing

4 swim

My picture dictionary → Go to page 91: Tick the words you know and trace.

5 **CD3 25** **Listen and circle the picture.**

1

2

3

4

6 **Look and write *can* or *can't*.**

1 I <u>can</u> run.　　　2 I _____ draw.

3 I _____ climb.　　4 I _____ dance.

7 **Look, read and tick ✓.**

1

Can you swim?

[ ] Yes, I can. [✓] No, I can't.

2

Can you jump?

[ ] Yes, I can. [ ] No, I can't.

3

Can you ride a bike?

[ ] Yes, I can. [ ] No, I can't.

4

Can you dance?

[ ] Yes, I can. [ ] No, I can't.

8 (About Me) **Complete the table. Ask three friends and tick ✓.**

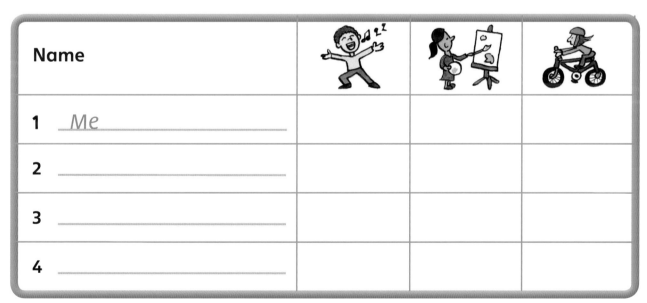

Name			
1 _Me_			
2			
3			
4			

(Can you sing?) (Yes, I can. / No, I can't.)

9 CD3 28 **Listen and number.**

a

b

c

d

e

f

1

10 **What's missing? Look and draw. Then stick.**

I help my friends.

a

b

c

11 **Trace the letters.**

An umbrella
bird can jump.

12 CD3 31 **Listen and circle the _u_ words.**

 1   2    3   4

What's the number?

1 Think and write the answer. Then colour.

1 1 + 1 = [2] red   **2** 2 + 4 = [ ] blue

3 3 + 6 = [ ] orange   **4** 10 − 2 = [ ] purple

5 5 − 2 = [ ] green   **6** 8 − 4 = [ ] yellow

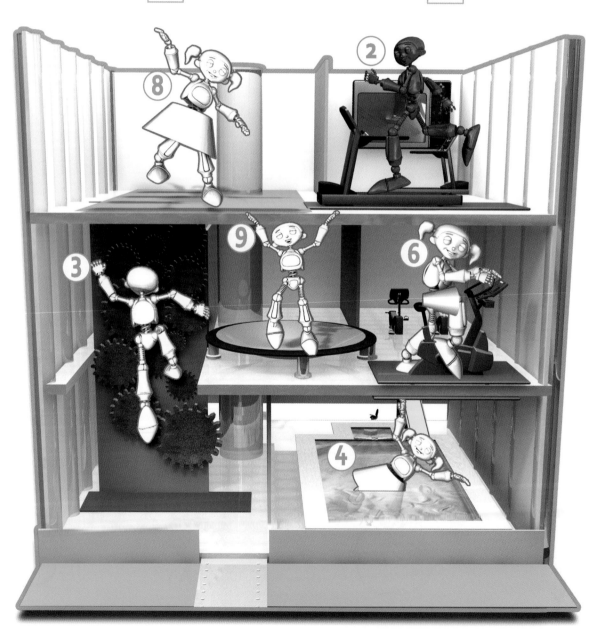

Evaluation

1 Look and write the word. Then read and say.

1. _r u n_

2. _ _ _ _ _

3. _ _ _ _ _ _

4. _ _ _ _ _

5. _ _ _ _

6. _ _ _ _

2 What's your favourite part? Use your stickers.

story   song   video

3 Puzzle Write the colour.

e y r g _____

Then go to page 93 and colour the Unit 7 pieces.

8 Animals

1 Look and match.

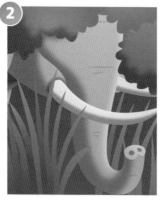
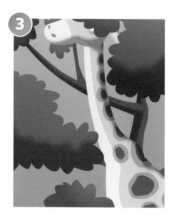

a crocodile **b** giraffe **c** spider **d** elephant

2 Look and write the word.

1  n l o i

lion

2  b e r z a

_____

3  i d b r

_____

4  o i p h p

_____

5  m y o e k n

_____

6  e a k n s

_____

3 (CD3 37) Listen and stick.

1	2	3

4	5	6

4 (Think) Write the words. Circle the animals with four legs.

snake   spider   bird   ~~zebra~~   elephant   giraffe   hippo   lion

1

zebra

2

3

4

5

6

7

8

My picture dictionary → Go to page 92: Tick the words you know and trace.

5 Look and match the opposites.

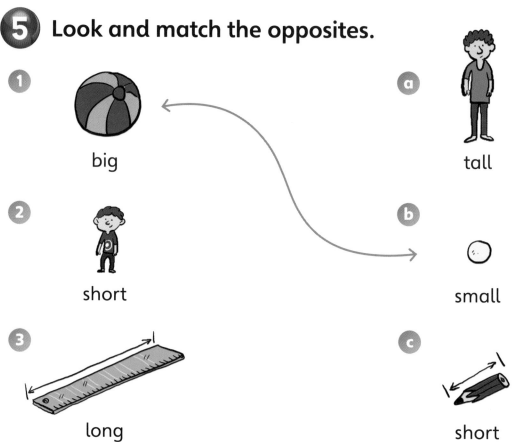

1 big

a tall

2 short

b small

3 long

c short

6 Look, read and complete the sentences.

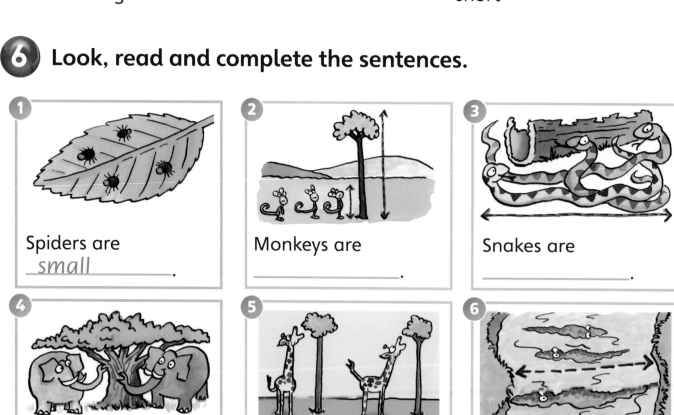

1 Spiders are _small_.

2 Monkeys are _____.

3 Snakes are _____.

4 Elephants are _____.

5 Giraffes are _____.

6 Baby crocodiles are _____.

7 **Look and read. Circle the correct sentences.**

1

Spiders have got wings.

2

Elephants have got long trunks.

3

Hippos have got long necks.

4

Monkeys have got long tails.

8 **Look and write.**

big teeth   long tails   ~~small wings~~   long necks   short legs

1   Birds have got _small_ _wings_ .

2   Zebras have got _____ _____ .

3   Hippos have got _____ _____ .

4   Giraffes have got _____ _____ .

5   Birds have got _____ _____ .

9 **Ask and answer with a friend.**

What are your favourite animals?   Elephants.

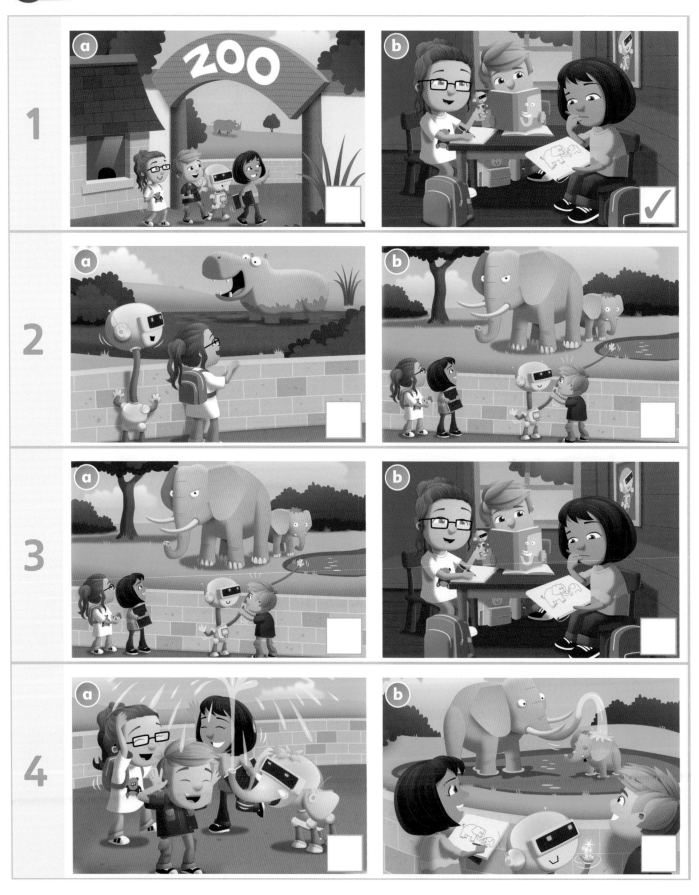

11 **What's missing? Look and draw. Then stick.**

I respect animals.

a

b

c

12 **Trace the letters.**

An octopus in an orange box.

13 CD3 46 **Listen and circle the o words.**

1

2

3

4

How do **animals** move?

1 **Read and complete. Then number the pictures.**

> slither   ~~walk~~   fly   walk

1 An elephant can ___walk___ .   **2** A snake can _____ .
3 A bird can _____ .   **4** A giraffe can _____ .

2 **Look at Activity 1 and circle the answers.**

1 Can a snake fly?   Yes, it can. / No, it can't.
2 Can an elephant walk?   Yes, it can. / No, it can't.
3 Can a bird fly?   Yes, it can. / No, it can't.
4 Can a giraffe slither?   Yes, it can. / No, it can't.

Evaluation

1 **Look and write the word. Then read and say.**

1. z e b r a
2. _ _ _ _
3. _ _ _ _ _
4. _ _ _ _ _ _ _ _
5. _ _ _ _ _ _ _
6. _ _ _ _

2  **What's your favourite part? Use your stickers.**

story   song   video

3 **Puzzle** **Write the colour.**

l c k a b _____

Then go to page 93 and colour the Unit 8 pieces.

Review Units 7 and 8

1 Look and write. Then draw number 9.

1. zebra
2. _ a _ _ o t a l
3. s _ a
4. j _ _
5. _ _ i _ p
6. _ _ n _ e
7. _ o _ e _
8. _ a n _

2 **Look and write.**

football   small   long necks   a bike   ~~swim~~

1 Can you _swim_ ?
2 Birds are _____ .
3 I can play _____ .
4 Giraffes have got _____ .
5 I can't ride _____ .

3 **Look, read and circle the words.**

1  (Snakes)/ **spiders** are long.

2 I **can** / **can't** sing.

3 Hippos **have got** / **haven't got** short tails.

4 I can **draw** / **dance**.

Hello!

blue ✓

green ☐

orange ☐

pink ☐

purple ☐

red ☐

yellow ☐

1 School

board ✓

book ☐

chair ☐

desk ☐

door ☐

pen ☐

pencil ☐

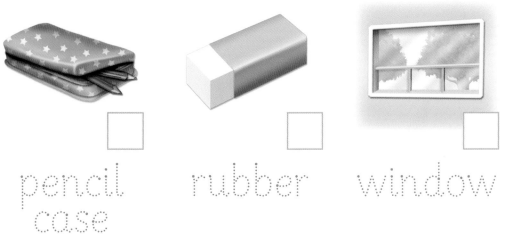

pencil case ☐

rubber ☐

window ☐

2 Toys

art set ✔

ball ☐

bike ☐

camera ☐

computer ☐

computer game ☐

doll ☐

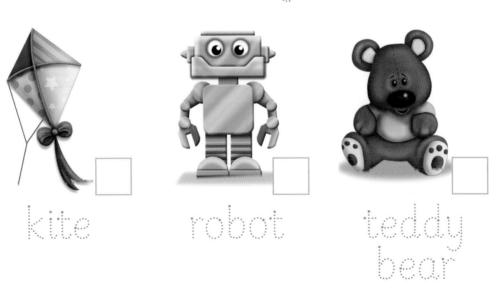

kite ☐

robot ☐

teddy bear ☐

(3) Family

aunt ✓

brother ☐

cousin ☐

dad ☐

grandma ☐

grandpa ☐

mum ☐

sister ☐

uncle ☐

4 At home

balcony ✓

bathroom

bedroom

dining room

flat

garden

hall

house

kitchen

living room

arms ✓

ears

eyes

feet

head

hair

hands

legs

mouth

nose

6 Food

apple ✓

banana ☐

bread ☐

cheese ☐

chicken ☐

egg ☐

juice ☐

milk ☐

orange ☐

water ☐

7 My actions

 ✓
climb

dance

draw

jump

paint

play
football

ride a
bike

run

sing

swim

8 Animals

bird ✓

crocodile ☐

elephant ☐

giraffe ☐

hippo ☐

lion ☐

monkey ☐

snake ☐

spider ☐

zebra ☐

My puzzle

Guess What!

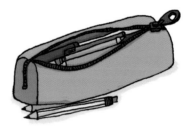

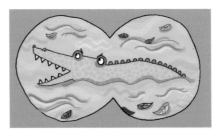